ION MUREŞAN
THE BOOK OF WINTER AND OTHER POEMS

Translated by Adam J. Sorkin
and Lidia Vianu

Featured Artist
Ciprian Paleologu

University of Plymouth Press

20 ROMANIAN WRITERS SERIES

Ion Mureşan's *The Book of Winter and Other Poems* is the tenth title to be published in the series 20 Romanian Writers by the University of Plymouth Press. The series is one aspect of the University of Plymouth's ongoing commitment to introduce Romania's vibrant artistic culture to other nations. In addition to the literature, the University of Plymouth is hosting a series of exhibitions and performances of Romania's visual and musical arts over five years to coincide with the publications. The following supplement features one of Romania's leading contemporary artists.

Featured Artist

CIPRIAN PALEOLOGU

Ciprian Paleologu (born 1976) studied painting at the University of Fine Arts, Bucharest, Romania. As a former pupil of Vasile Grigore he gained his PhD under the supervision of Gheorghe Achiţei. He is currently a lecturer at the National University of Arts, Bucharest, he has been Exhibitions Department Manager to the Romanian Artists Association and is now also the Curator for the Romanian Painting Exhibition, Tokyo Metropolitan Art Space Exhibition Gallery. Paleologu is a member of the Artists Union of Romania. His first exhibition was in 1996 – 'Dominvs', Dominvs Gallery, Bucharest – and he has been prolific ever since with exhibitions in Russia, France, Italy, Turkey, Greece, Estonia and Serbia. Paleologu's topics revolve around human understanding mechanisms which spring from the superficial to the deepest understanding. Paleologu's Human project – 24 exhibitions every two years over the life span of a human being, like Mureşan, is a homage to powerlessness with eventual promise of salvation.

Awards include the 2007 'Margareta Sterian' Prize from the Romanian National Art Museum for the best contemporary art exhibition for 2006 and in 2008, second prize in the International Painting Competition, Florean Museum, Baia Mare, Romania.

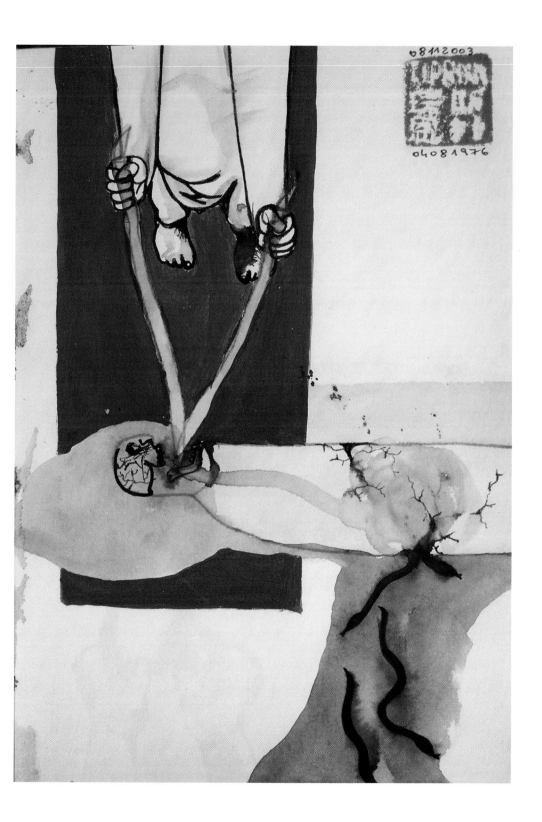

AB IRATO

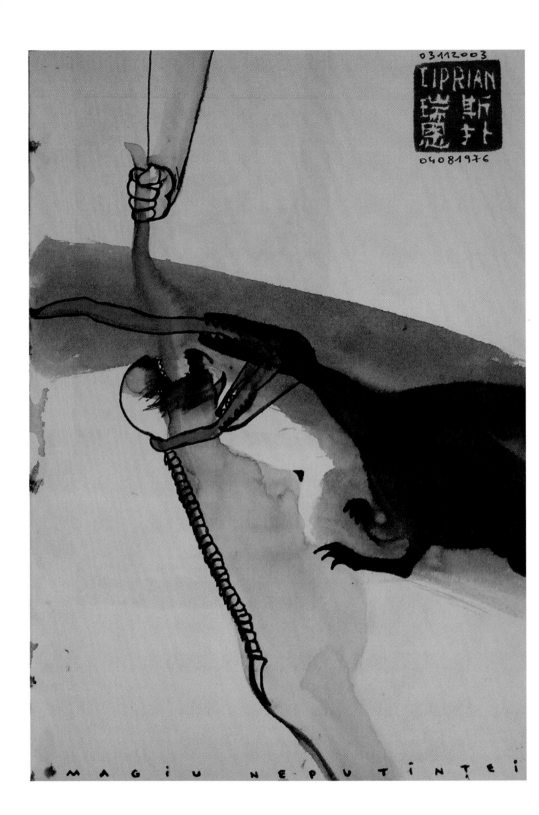

MAGIU NEPUTINTEI

HOMINEM QUAERO

NON DECET

TERRA IGNOTA

OMAGIU NEPUTINTEI (2003)

INCOGNITO

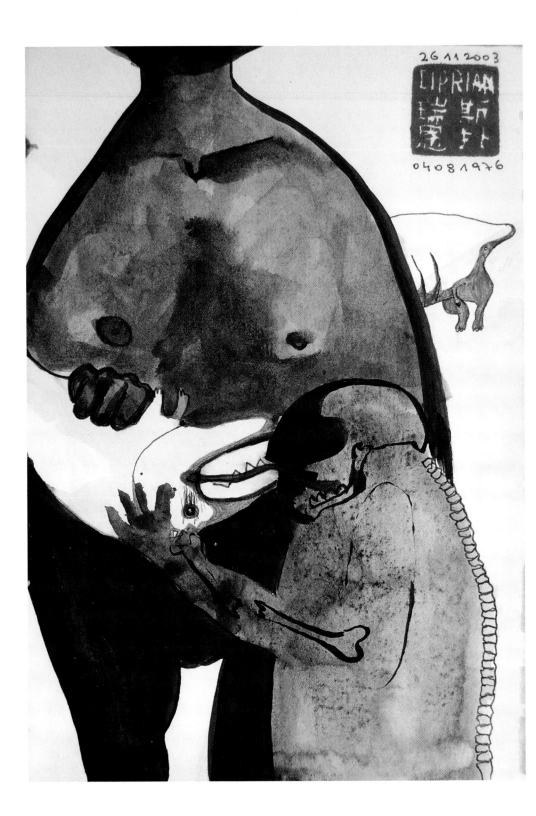

MORE MAJORUM

DURA NECESSITAS

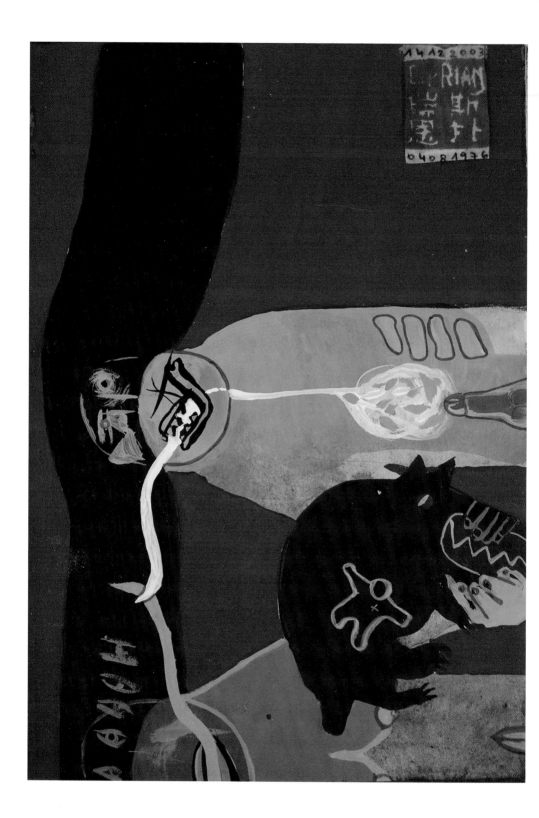

GLORIA VICTIS

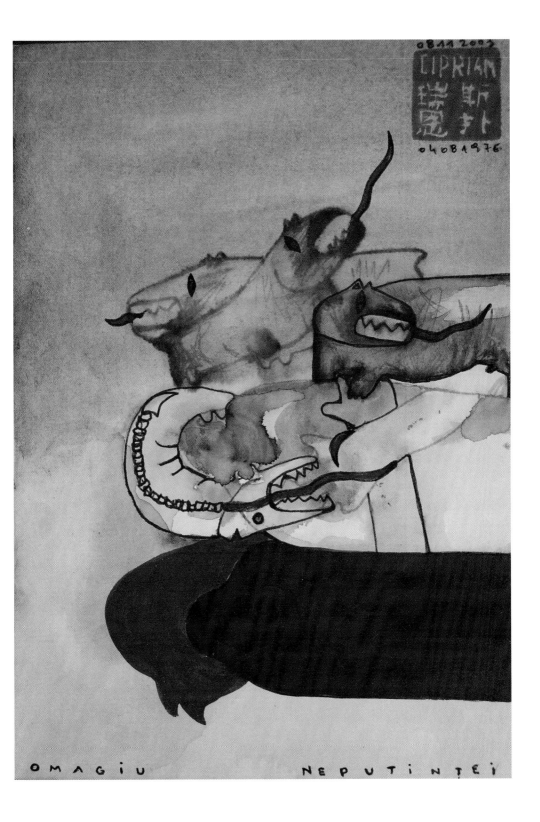

OMAGIU   NEPUTINȚEI

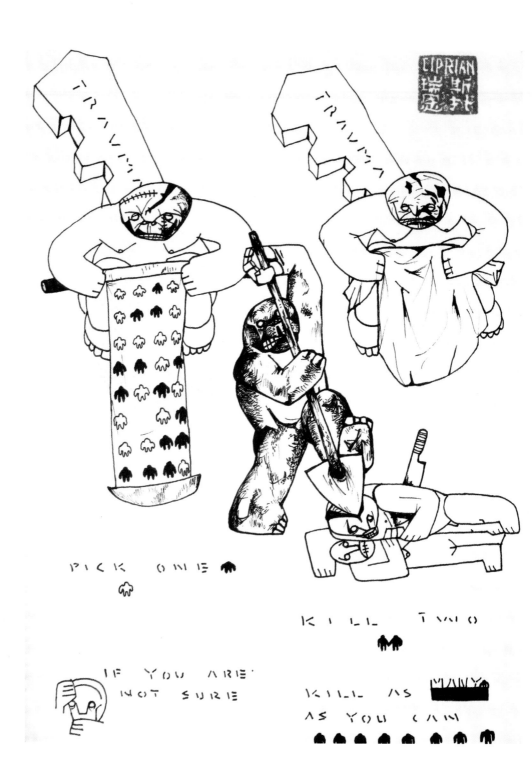

TRAUMA

BUT i STILL
HAVE
MY

MEA CULPA

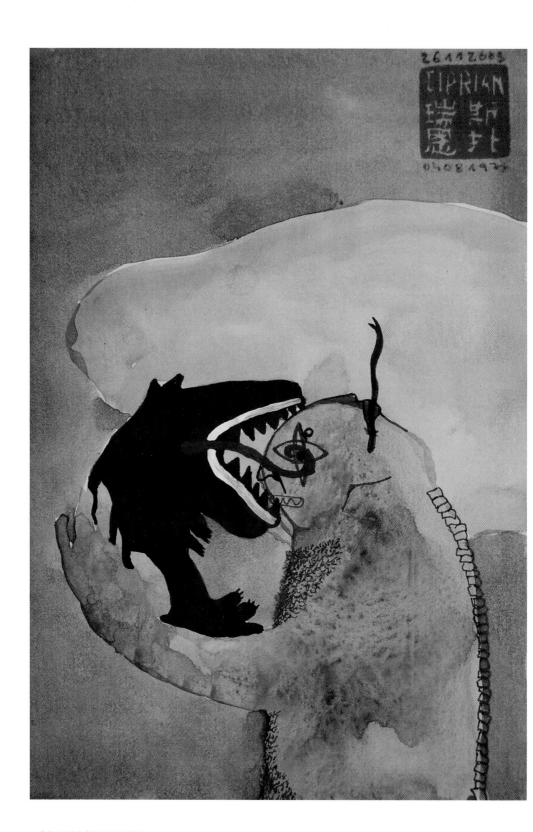

COMPESCE MENTEM

INITIIS OBSTA

OMAGIU   NEPUTINȚEI

SAPERE AUDE

ION MUREȘAN
THE BOOK OF WINTER AND OTHER POEMS

Translated by Adam J. Sorkin
and Lidia Vianu

Contents

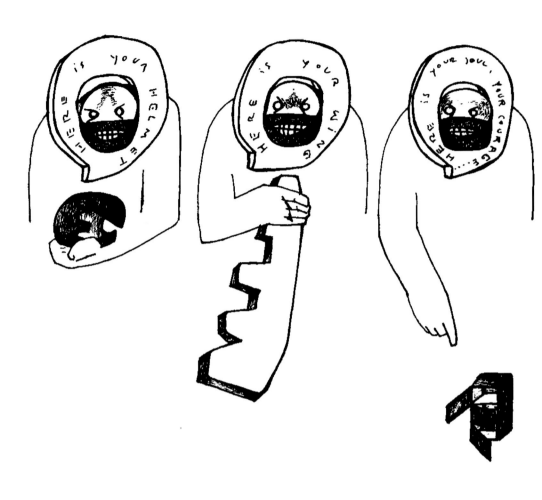

SPEAKING WITH
MY LEFT FOOT

Adam J. Sorkin

Introducing
Ion Mureșan

I Sing the Dark Force in My Mind

"I sing the dark force in my mind," writes Ion Mureşan in a recent poem, 'Dark Song.' It's a kind of poetic credo, one of a number of moments when the poet speaks directly about poetry and the world its writers and readers live in – directly, but not necessarily as simply as may first seem. Mureşan's work is challenging, even to fellow poets and admiring literary critics, let alone to the willingly engaged reader. His lyrical discourse is often cerebral, hermetic, convoluted: "I am the dark force in the mind of the dark force in my mind," this same poem elaborates, near its end. The characteristic imagery of his poetry, always precise in detail, shifts without transition between the sensory world of everyday actuality and an irrational, dream-like (occasionally nightmarish) terrain of the surreal, fantastic, absurd, even oracular.

Both polarities in this dichotomy come across in the poems as equally real. "I have only one prejudice – reality," begins 'The Expulsion from Poetry,' but what "reality" is, whether outward or inward, physical or mental, the cognisant here and now, the remembered past, or the anticipated future, becomes blurred, a suspension of judgement, 'slippery' in its articulation, though neither the question nor Mureşan's poetry ever loses its fascination or vivid aesthetic presence. An inspired poetic madness is rarely far away from the poet's attention: "I tell myself that I should show more indulgence of my own madness," 'The Poem of Winter' confides, ending, "I rise up from my armchair / and begin to bark. 'Woof woof woof.'" The visionary intensity and impressionistic subjectivity modify to a degree in Mureşan's most recent book, which I'll comment on below, but the poetry never deviates from its concentration on the poet's mediation between world and spirit, self and word, emotion and interpretation: "I speak from inside my skin… / offering words a kind of dignity with pores and delicate downy hair."

Ion Mureşan is not just self-conscious but also self-mocking and playful about the challenges of his writing. In a riddling phrase that serves as the title of the poem I'm about to quote from (and of the book it appears in, Mureşan's second collection), the poetic persona announces that he is working on "the poem that cannot be understood" and immediately specifies, "It's a shiny black rock" – polished, beautiful, sensual, revelatory of an unyielding quality, elemental, and a bit frightening. Another poem, 'The Poem on Poetry' from Mureşan's first book, begins, "All my life I have gathered rags to make a scarecrow"; however, this five-line confession concludes, "Yet now that it's ready, night after night I turn off the light and simply suspecting it's there, / I start to howl in terror." Perhaps the fear derives, and cannot be separated, from the essential reality, poetry's intrinsic nature. 'The Poem That Cannot Be Understood' ends with a more hopeful (possibly illusory) vision of poetry's capacity to move and change its readers: "getting old, nearly hunchbacked,… / I stand in line, behind hundreds and hundreds of people, / in order to see, at least at the end of my days, / the poem that heals, / the poem that cannot be understood."

Ion Mureșan was born on January 9, 1955, in Vultureni, a village in the county of Cluj in Transylvania, the region of Romania where he has spent his entire career. His parents were peasants. Educated at Babeș–Bolyai University of Cluj, he graduated with a degree in philosophy. While at university, he became a member of the group centred on the influential literary review *Echinox;* then after graduation, part of a writers' circle, Sæculum, that formed in Cluj, migrated to Dej (where the communist authorities closed it), and then found sanctuary (or at least was ignored by the powers that be) in the village of Beclean in northern Transylvania. In 1981, Mureșan was assigned to teach history in a primary school in the isolated village of Strâmbu, which he did until 1988, when he returned to Cluj as editor of the venerable cultural magazine, *Tribuna.* As he later observed in an interview, commenting on the state 'model' for treating writers as potential threats in the 1980s, "we were in practise all spread out, sent the devil knows where… so that we could not gather, it was a communist obsession that organisations not be created, that there not be organised structures." After the 1989 revolution that overthrew the communist government, Mureșan continued as a journalist in Cluj, as editor-in-chief of *Verso,* a cultural magazine.

Meanwhile Mureșan gained increasing prestige for his poetry and his role as a cultural celebrity. Although very active in public festivals, debates, readings, panels, and the like, in producing books of his poetry he is decidedly restrained, a craftsman with a sensibility seemingly possessed by a pure quest for literary perfection. "I do not make poetry by the kilogram," he said in an interview. Indeed, his three collections of poetry, published at widely spaced intervals – *The Book of Winter (Cartea de iarnă,* 1981), *The Poem That Cannot Be Understood (Poemul care nu poate fi înțeles,* 1993), and *The Alcohol Book (Cartea Alcool,* 2010) – would not weigh in at half that. He has written a book of short stories, *The Sunday of Madness (Duminica turbării,*

1994). His collection of essays on revisiting books he read as a child, *The Lost Book – a Poetics of Traces* (*Cartea pierdută – o poetică a urmei*, 1998), was honoured by the Cluj branch of the Romanian Writers' Union. In 2004, he published *Carnival in the Meadow* (*Carnavalul din poiană*, written with his wife Ana), a book of plays for children that also won similar recognition. Along the way, Mureşan poems were published in literary magazines and some of his work reprinted in anthologies, including a collection of five poets of the Romanian 1980s who ran counter to the decade's fashionable dogma of elaborate post-modernist irony and intertextuality, *The Absinth Drinkers* (*Băutorii de absint*, edited by Bogdan Creţu, 2007).

Some of Mureşan's poems have been translated into English (in my own co-translations with others) in *Transylvanian Voices: An Anthology of Contemporary Poets of Cluj-Napoca* (1994; revised and enlarged, 1997), and *Day After Night: Twenty Romanian Poets for the Twenty-First Century* (1999). Two books of his work were published in French, *Le mouvement sans coeur de l'image* (2001), and in a bilingual German-Romanian edition, *Zugang verboten / Acces interzis* (2008). In 2005, he was invited to France under the programme Les Belles Étrangères. There is also a trilingual volume containing one poem that Lidia Vianu and I independently selected and co-translated for this University of Plymouth Press collection, *Paharul / Glass / Au fond de verre* (2007).

Mureşan is a member of the Romanian Writers' Union and is a founding member of the Association of Professional Writers of Romania (ASPRO).

The year Mureşan graduated from university also saw his first collection of poetry, *The Book of Winter* (*Cartea de iarnă*, published in Bucharest by the distinguished Cartea Românească [The Romanian Book] publishing house). Included in its entirety here, *The Book of Winter* won a Romanian Writers' Union prize for a debut volume of poetry, and in the view of many critics it is one of the most important books of the 1980s. Mureşan thus appeared on the scene at the beginning of Romania's bleakest decade – communism's last stand, as it were – which was manifested in widespread restrictions on fundamental liberties and scarcities of basics and amenities both, with a lack of heating resulting from planned shortages of fuel, and a freeze on individual expression of thought in a context of political and social repression. The same decade featured, in contrast, the experimentalism and the flagrant stylistic games of the 'blue-jeans' generation of poets, Mureşan's contemporaries, who broke with previous Romanian artistic modalities. Mureșan, himself much more of a traditional modernist and expressionist than an iconoclast or, in the self-description of a prominent 1990s group, a 'fracturist', nonetheless seems in retrospect to have struck just the right note with his book's title. It is not surprising that in a recent interview Mureșan stressed that "the poet's social role is essential" – by which he means, as he went on to say, "I have often maintained that poets are the right medicine for this ill society."

The Book of Winter can be said to foreshadow the harsh period during the 1980s, when such famous incidents occurred (in the way I've heard the anecdote) as the time a Romanian audience, huddled in their winter coats, hats, scarves, and gloves in an unheated theatre for a performance of Shakespeare's *Richard III*, applauded the opening line, "Now is the winter of our discontent,…" choosing to hear it as a veiled political barb. In fact, Mureșan's poetry, for the most part, neither glares forth with the pop-culture-savvy verbal gamesmanship of Romania's post-modernism-before-post-communism (the most prominent example is the poet and prose writer Mircea Cărtărescu) nor positions itself as the repository of parabolic, black-humour, between-the-lines hints at resistance to censorship and the party-state, such as was achieved in referential camouflage by a number of poets popular both in Romania and in the West more for their implicit dissident politics than for their otherwise strong, personally moving and/or witty poetry (*e.g.*, Ana Blandiana, Mircea Dinescu, or Marin Sorescu). However, a few of Mureșan's allusions in the poems certainly would have been read as subversive, such as the parodic language of civil obedience in happily respecting traffic lights or the inclusion of an otherwise unidentified "Elena" twice, a name that, whether intended by the author or not, Romanian readers would almost automatically have associated with dictator Nicolae Ceaușescu's reviled wife.

Instead, in *The Book of Winter* and the volumes that followed it, the figure of the poet is presented with a more complex and elevated conception than as an imp of protest, rather in a priestly aspect – which in effect turns out to be the same thing as the pose of a madman. *The Book of Winter* is arranged in four sections, the first three numbered and the last presented somewhat disingenuously as merely an 'Addenda,' although it contains the tellingly named five-part sequence, 'The Expulsion from Poetry.' Images of cold and lunacy suffuse the book, alongside images of being laid bare: "Anyhow, I stand before my poetic creed as before a woman without skin...." The poet's "flesh my yellow flesh" is "winter's cruellest coming" in a refrain in his bitterly ironic 'As for Beauty.' While the collection contains much that one might call beauty in its language and fluid imagery as well as raw emotional power, it is notable that Mureşan chooses to close the book with lines personifying madness as it "sits at my work table," leading the poet, whose verbal costumes and masks reflect a kaleidoscopic means of confronting and making spiritual an alien, tragic, deformed, problematic reality, to want to assume still another, familiarly paradoxical poetic guise, that of a kind of prophet, and "to scream with somebody else's mouth, even a deaf mute's."

Winter suggests a frozen season as dangerous as a poetic state, a deathly condition. Poetry itself is an affliction – "I just carry my disease: this poem / like a sour apple in my mouth" – albeit a saving affliction. But if winter is ultimately associated with death, both poetry and madness are possible means of transcendence, and there is something religious about them. Without them, as Mureşan warns in the book's opening poem, "we shall not be pardoned."

Twelve years after his first book, *The Poem That Cannot Be Understood* (*Poemul care nu poate fi înţeles*) appeared in Târgu Mureş in 1993 and went on to win critical acclaim as well as the poetry prize of the Romanian Writers' Union. The volume extends and deepens Mureşan's literary exploration of the fears, neuroses, and displacements that constitute his persona's interior reality. The voice of these carefully wrought, ambitious poems is perhaps more openly ironic, and the imagery even more extraordinary, intense, and varied. The poet is very much like a conjurer whose art transforms what he thinks and says into unfamiliar objects, a kind of magician depicted as if a "very old man yelling something incomprehensible" and evoking "fear" that causes others to band together and stand vigil. The poet excoriates poetry as "poisonous" and goes on to accuse it: "you have exhausted my life, squandered the honey of my days...." As critics have defined Mureşan's work, the tonalities are 'fiery,' the poetry 'metaphysical.' On the other hand, to the writer, poetry is likewise communication, connection, "white cartilage stretched taut from mouth to mouth," and it is God's revelation that, within it, "the spirit" looks back, "grinning from the brain's periphery." The seven poems from *The Poem That Cannot Be Understood* translated and included here in *The Book of Winter and Other Poems* were selected by the poet himself.

After a wait of 17 years, Mureșan's much anticipated third book of new poems, *The Alcohol Book* (*Cartea Alcool*), was launched in 2010, to instant acclaim. Named best poetry volume of the year with an award from the Romanian Ministry of Culture, the book is somewhat of a departure for Mureșan in that numbers of poems are narrative and discursive, relatively transparent, with what one might call an avatar of the poet, "the bearded man," appearing as a character in several of them, whereas a first-person voice guides others. The mood and themes, not unexpectedly, display a consistency with Mureșan's two earlier books (the phrase I use for the title of this introduction, from the poem 'Dark Song,' was borrowed from *The Alcohol Book*). In the collection, Mureșan gives new prominence to the subject matter signalled by the title (which alludes biographically to his own drinking but also associates itself with the mystical alcohol of French symbolist and surrealist traditions, particularly in the imagination of Rimbaud and Apollinaire). The pub, or bar, or the drinker's glass, becomes holy lyrical terrain, just as the alcoholics of 'The Alcoholics' Poem' seem to have a special communication with God, along with a sort of specially protected innocence. Mureșan has said explicitly, "Sometimes I wonder if you don't find God in a pub rather than in a church." In a 2011 interview on Romanian television, reprinted in *Tribuna*, he noted, "I am a religious person, a religious man, and I believe that, in the end, and I've said this many times before, poetry is the best proof of God's existence."

The Alcohol Book contains 32 poems. "You could ask me why 32," Mureșan suggested, co-opting his interviewer's role, and then proceeded to answer, "There were more poems, but I stopped at 33 and removed one.… So there wouldn't be 33, Christ's age." The collection has instances of tenderness that coexist with self-mockery and a mature acceptance of the cruel, the evil, and the sordid; at the same time the poetry indicates a sense of wonder at the world, a love for it. In the simple, child-like poem 'The Glass,' the speaker may fall, like Lewis Carroll's Alice, except not down a rabbit hole, but into a tumbler of vodka, with pain and tears, yet this Song of Experience rather charmingly turns into a kind of Song of Innocence with its half-reassuring, though also half-ironic, refrain, 'All is dream and harmony.' And in the moment of fear and conjoined anger and weakness after the narrative of events in 'The Old Lover and the Young Lady,' more of a love poem with religious overtones than might first seem, the first-person voice of the poem reacts to his 'lady' momentarily with resentment, but immediately he relents: "And I call her slut. But then angel."

The poems included here from *The Alcohol Book* were selected by the translators, to round out the English-language reader's view of Ion Mureșan's talent and to bring this collection up to date.

THE BOOK OF WINTER
AND OTHER POEMS

THE BOOK OF WINTER
(1981)

I

The Voice

The sister's solitary voice crossed the rooms.
I'm not an adept at voluptuousness, but I touch things
as I would touch a woman's thighs. For we shall not be pardoned.
Soon we shall see with a bird's vision
above huge heaps of fruit.

The sister's solitary voice crossed the rooms.
This dark throne in the middle of the plantation,
and the poet is like a slate-blue pond in autumn –
his strength far away from him.

Carts of Sugar Cane

Then the child heard the Master
inventing the lyre beside the Red Sea.
A red song hides in the polecats' den.

At dusk the Master is borne on a green litter
across the glassy mountains and the peacock
sojourns among cattle merchants, teaching them:

"Let the poem wait forty days more…"

A long way off, desert dwellers stab the sheep,
set sugar cane carts ablaze under archways of mahogany.

There nobody foretells the peacock's death
(only the seed of clean animals will whirl itself into foam).

Cold

At the far reaches of memory it's so cold that
if a swan were shot
an old man could inhabit the wound.

At the far reaches of memory it's so cold that
the neighbours merely stand waist deep in sawdust and sing,
the neighbours – like greenish flames.

The Glorious Gardens of Gold

With great cunning beauty pounced on me,
like a rabid bitch beauty pounced on me.
"Let everyone perish with his wealth," I proclaim,
and rolling my eyes, as dry as the wood of a tree struck by lightning,
I roar with laughter at elegant, complicated ceremonies
and recite silly ditties.

With great cunning beauty pounced on me –
the principles of power are beguiling
but everything else, no more than boredom.
Hey, we're going to lay a poisoned trap
in the glorious gardens of gold.

Let everyone perish with his wealth –
sober meals, two or three exotic fruits on a silver tray,
no more joy than words,
the ridiculous trajectories of cutlery in the stuffy air
the stubborn words that can no longer be peeled
and a vision of the century gliding beneath the window's gloom:
a marble terrace as broad as a plain, at the far end of which
is a mercenary all but invisible disappearing into the distance,
bent over more and more,
his ever stranger footsteps scarcely as loud as a whisper.

About the Construction of a Huge Shed

This morning I take my rest in the silver armchair.
Under the yellowed house wall I talk about you shyly
and say: here's the dark red wine
I promised you.

This morning I take my rest in the silver armchair
and I'm on the point of thinking: in this dusty season the friend's gardens
are submerged under a clear water…
And next: about the arduous construction of a huge shed
on the shore of the sea.

A Loud Burst of Laughter

At parties I've seen eyes redder than fox fur
– this is about women's gossip women's gossip –
I won't hurt you I won't tell the truth
I just carry my disease: this poem
like a sour apple in my mouth.

At parties I've seen eyes redder than fox fur
– this is about women's gossip women's gossip.
About my love: she hears a loud burst of laughter underground.
Her eyes like abandoned mud-baths that
gleam for you like verdigrised metal in the night,
esteemed gentlemen beautiful ladies young maidens.

A Ladder Leaning Against a Tower

North of the city in a stone quarry we sang tunelessly.
  We sang: I remember I remember wild-animal skins fluttering on the building,
    the sun was setting, a pale white pub had begun to burn with high flames
      and it was then we received the tidings
        that a child had slipped out through a window
          and kept floating hours above the outskirts.

North of the city in a stone quarry we sang awkwardly.
  I could tell you a widow's tale: a red ladder leaning against a tower
    then in an eddy of wind and leaves
      he arrived from the distant verge of the plain
        and a voice could be heard in the dusk
          crying out across the expanse, "Dog dog…"

But can you believe me when not so very long ago
  at the end of one of your long trips you found me
    drunk, stretched out on a glass table,
      in a snow-covered valley among mountains?

As for Beauty

My flesh my yellow flesh
I think of as you as of winter's cruellest coming.
My strength freezes my hands.
My strength freezes my heart.

Every cruel thing has been spoken
and for an entire lifetime I've brought news to a friend:
God's laundered scarves scarcely can protect
from rain and melancholy.

My flesh my yellow flesh,
I think of as you as of winter's cruellest coming.

As for the illumination of large buildings
with tallow candles – it is so.
As for beauty: the only way of doing without it
is to do its bidding.
At wise men's feasts under their tables
amidst their feet, I continue unimpeded
my hysterical game with blue pebbles.

My flesh my yellow flesh,
I think of as you as of winter's cruellest coming.

II

for Petru

The Poem on Poetry

All my life I have gathered rags to make a scarecrow.
I remember the days when hidden under the bed I perfected my work
the heap of old shoes I would sometimes lay my head on when I fell asleep.
Yet now that it's ready, night after night I turn off the light and simply
        suspecting it's there,
I start to howl in terror.

The Sign

The imbecile air of an affair in weather like this when
at any movement the blood in your body jangles like a necklace of gold
        coins.
Then the idea: would it be useful if your breasts had windows
or anyway some sort of dormer windows? The top floor
of the hospital for professional diseases bows almost imperceptibly
over a yellow petal.
Here and there, a plump hand slips out through a crack in the wall
and rests limp on the pavement.
Refresh your memory, then: "From your kind I'll make
a hazy vapour rise, it'll do no harm
but be good like false news."
"A ritual washing" – behold your face
scissored out of mouse fur.
Cling to this sign: when the sun climbs high above the butcher shop
and takes on the same hue as an ocean fish's belly,
you can hear equally well with an ear of hip flesh
or an ear of head flesh.

Out the Window

If we ever reach the city
you too will see the shutters open wide
and women throwing into the streets supper's leftovers of angel wings.

The Poem of Winter

I

Ay, not even the works of the gods are as wondrous as a great culture in
      decline.
The perverted hermaphroditic forms multiply like cancer cells,
all winter you can watch them by the fireplace in a frenzy of rut
and even experience sensual delight peering into your microscope.
"So finical, so finical," I exclaim, and with moist lips kiss my death on its
      little muzzle.
All alone, I hurriedly conceal myself in a horse's skin and climb to the
      window,
passers-by will see a solitary horse in a window.
At last I tell myself that I should show more indulgence of my own
      madness.
I describe my fight with the dog's image: teeth grind in the photographic
      paper,
oh, I've managed to bite off an ear. Mother and father have climbed to the
      attic
to watch the fight. "Glory, glory," they shout, shedding tears of joy.
They hear my teeth grind in the photographic paper. I open my mouth
      and let them see
the sign of my power: a narrow streak of blood mixed with spittle.
Yeah, yeah, love of nature. Look at him, he's made a fish hatchery in his
      own blood.
Love of nature doesn't usually leave visible traces,
but for you there's no room in childhood for hairy legs.
Measles chickenpox hives could at best arouse vague erotic sensations…
(Swallow your words show respect now lie face down!)
"My mouth's crooked, my mouth's crooked, my mouth's crooked," I keep
      repeating to myself –
so I have to believe it tomorrow out of regard for the memory.
For God's sake, I mustn't forget to kiss Miss Elena's hands,
those trembling hands that seem always to be wringing a bird's neck.
(Lie face down swallow your words show respect!)

II

The matriarchate has come to an end.
I did many a good deed while it lasted.
Now it's Saturday afternoon it's cold and I've nothing left to think about.
The beautiful lady goes on crying on my shoulder.

"Praise be all commercial transactions,"
I stammer and tally the hours gone by.
"The most wondrous of birds is the God of Commerce.
Tomorrow morning we'll start to tame the wild animals."

"Let's squander the old gentleman's fortune."
The children's choir sings at the edge of a forest,
Faces staring at the fabulous city until
Their teeth glow pink as rose petals.

III

As much decorum as a dead man deserves in winter,
after a frosty night his pupils become flowers of ice, a splendour.
Still, we can admire the form of the naked body in the snow
balanced on scales that, right this instant,
take a look, a reddish dog is curling up on. Ultimately talking by the flame
        of a candle
is like talking at the mouth of a cave. Even better a cosy tea party:
the white head of your neighbour seems to grow directly from the wood of
        the table,
"When I feel anger, I feel destiny," he says, "like anger, really, but much
        stronger."
One fine day you glance in the mirror and see something like a mist rising
        over a swamp,
then you live contented because you have seen your own voice.
(Pick up a pen and scribble a quick accounting on the dead man's belly…)
I'm so lonely that I can imagine what it would feel like if I kissed a spider
and I can imagine it's so cold words shatter in the mouth,
brittle like stones in deserts. Even better a cosy tea party
at which I furtively sniff my armpits like plants protected by law,
and I practise praising the china.
In her colourful ballroom gown Elena opens the door as she would pry
        open
a dog's mouth. "Woof woof." I rise up from my armchair
and begin to bark. "Woof woof woof."

Ascension to the Skies

I speak from inside my skin, the only thing that spurs my ambition to take
        things as they come,
offering words a kind of dignity with pores and delicate downy hair
(exactly what at ten I endowed the baby snake with, after it had suddenly
        struck from inside my chest
and I felt its cool head between my lips.
My sister clapped her hands merrily supposing I'd suddenly managed to
        speak
a black word with eyes:
"Look, Mummy, what long words foreign languages have!"
Then the same snake in the tin bowl rustling like a book printed on cheap
        paper).
Some spiritual phenomenon or another gets lost, while
some organ or another doesn't get lost, yet
naked and fearful, I hug my body in the mirror.
But what could I do with two voices in my mouth?
No doubt at this moment I'm strolling through the city with my dignity
        bundled on a stick over my shoulder.
I jab a finger in my consciousness as easily as in a jar of yogurt
and stir till it gets soft, soft, soft.
In broad daylight a man stands scratching his head thoughtfully and spits
        into his memory as into an abandoned well:
"Memory?" As though I'd been greedy enough to long for eyelids with
        fangs and molars
so I could chew my eyes all day!
We shall see this man later toward the end of this poem
in the guise of a swarm of fruit flies (*Drosophila melanogaster*)
as he limps through the gates of culture.
Anyhow, I stand before my poetic creed as before a woman without skin
who powders her veins, and if I sometimes kiss her, am I any better than
the butcher who, after closing his shop, buries his tear-streaked face in the
        joints of meat
left unsold?
Let's say I insert my neck between object and cause,
let's say my neck stays between poem and its cause

like a woman's uterus between spermatozoon and egg.

And if my friends boast that an ear has grown on their belly, they should
      be talked to

by bellies. I know them too well: they keep a kernel of truth in their
      mouths

and suck it like a sweet.

I counted and counted: I have more knuckles than fingers.

Of late I receive bundles of mail urging me to decide at what age to go
      mad.

Hey, hey, tomorrow morning I'll catch a reddish dog by the leg and
      whirling it round over my head like a propeller,

surely I must ascend to the skies.

Here is what I always have known: those who confess their power do so
      with the stench of a barren animal.

Here is what I have learned: while still a child it was foretold I was
      destined for something important,

then in primary school letters blossomed on paper like measles,

tiny, playful animals changing colour on my classmate's face.

"Last summer I visited the city where I had the opportunity to walk
      around a lot

in order to obey the traffic laws. Oh, how deeply moved I was

to cross the streets in due conformity with the signals on the traffic
      lights…"

Ay, body of mine, so this is how you preserve yourself in the world like a
      multicolour collation boiling in a precious kettle!

And right at this moment my judgment bleeds over my sole image of
      spiritual peace:

a fair-haired soldier combing his hair in the small harmless windows of the
      bathhouse.

Hey, hey, tomorrow morning I'll catch a reddish dog by the leg and
      whirling it round over my head like a propeller,

surely I must ascend to the skies.

Kynos Kephalai

for Iulia-Monica

I

Posterity has no time for revisions and beauty never hinders sales.
The dogs' heads tattooed on your knees will make a good impression
at the gala, I can tell you – I, the Beast, "he who chooses his words
with particular care and when he speaks the air breaks out in angry red
        blisters
as if he were speaking with his head underwater." "An experiment
        conducted with a singular
sensibility, gentlemen: admire these purebred dogs,
with what calm and refinement they lick and bite one another, like two
philosophical concepts," you say, the very same thing you also said about
        the First
World War. *Kynos kephalai Kynos kephalai*, hurry,
hurry, under an orange parasol the card game has begun
in the garden. And I, the Beast, will begin my poem
praising each of you for your beautiful death.

II

It's hard to be ready all the time, to bear in mind your good clothes
(my clothes are secretly my meanness).
Oho! and the guests had a herky-jerky way of dancing like
a child's abrupt movements when he secretly undresses his doll,
cuts up her colourful belly with scissors, *sees* that piece of cloth
tightly covering a handful of loose tow…
In memory your own face is the vaguest detail:

Euchloris smaragdaria

a splotch of greenish, somewhat denser air on a colour plate with bright
      butterflies.
Dressed in our good clothes, then, we admire our long legs stretched out
      on the fresh grass,
words swell up and begin to be born in the mouth,
hands turn red, redder than the heart.

III

We mourn over your body
(just like the Greeks when plague devastated flourishing cities),
that cannot find room in this poem and swings with every gust of wind
like a suicide on a rope or like those cinched under the bellies of sheep
when they divine Sunday coming
and, fleece in their eyes, rejoice without seeing…
Alas alas my little blue coronet lost in the weeds.
I baited you with birdlime, oh my death,
the most perfect mannequin for the city's renowned houses of
            haute couture.

IV

Counting moles on our body we pay close attention to their growing
and shrinking, and we rejoice at the flourish of constellations on our back,
we exult before autumnal reflections of that one strand of hair among the
        others
whose auspicious growth we have lovingly tended since adolescence,
or we dwell on the sloughs of vision
where a multitude of trifles gambol and blend their colours, etc.

• *excerpts from the secret reports we sent to dog breeders*

…in her breast winter can be heard as it comes…
the smell of roses will still reign in the cages…
for a few days there will a bustling among the animals as intense
as the half hour before dinner…
…animal cemeteries will be dug up,
dogs fed the vertebrae of lambs…
…we understand that the orbit betrays the planet…
…*Kynos kephalai Kynos kephalai* hurry hurry
under an orange parasol the card game
has begun in the garden…

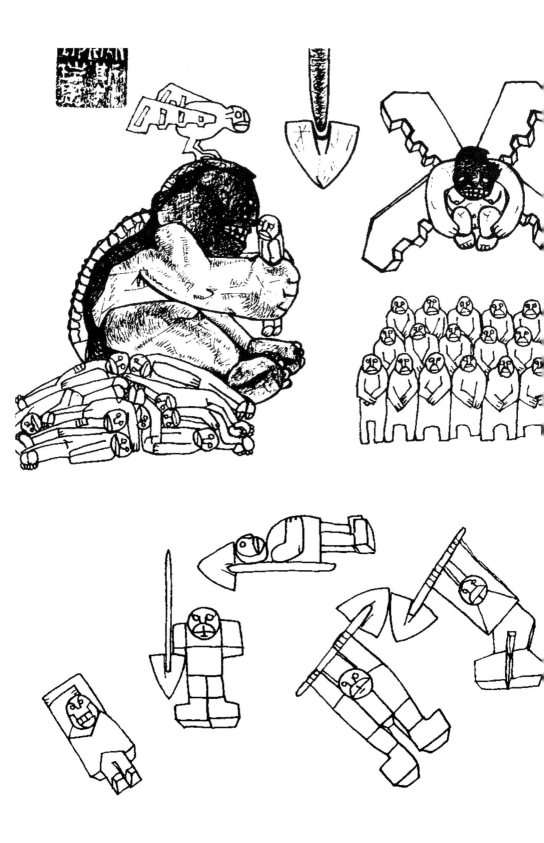

Self-Portrait as a Child

You must stick to practical things, Father.
I shall tag along with the madmen to pick coltsfoot on the riverbanks.
I must preserve memory distinct from order,
covering it in red sand.

You must stick to practical things, Father.
I shall live in the attic and drink strong wine.
I must describe the sharp fantastic sound that echoes
when the name clangs against the thing it names.

You must stick to practical things, Father.
I shall dance gracefully and see in my dream
street lamps of shadow.

The One Who Paints the Hill

Children bent low over the vessel of dark water,
clad in glassy cloaks in high-ceilinged cellars.
Also bent low over the vessel of dark water now
is the one who paints the hill blue.

Children clad in glassy cloaks everywhere in the house.
You can see the golden door through which the lone buffalo
ventures out into the streets. The feast begins above the city –
frozen wine stains on Mother's brow.

Children clad in glassy cloaks – speak, Sister –
frozen wine stains discolour your brow.
Under the floor foul rats – speak, Sister –
the one who paints the scythe from the hill that's blue
draws ever nearer, mounting the brown stair.

Mountain Sanatorium

In sleep I keep watch on the burning hut
the lady embracing a tree-trunk of alcohol
the yellow windows of fear opening in the thorn hedge.
With my whole body I stroke the womb of colours.

In sleep I keep watch on the burning hut
the thread of stone thick as the horse's body
passing straight fantastically straight through the forest
the lady's laughter in the stream's steep falls.

In sleep I keep watch on the burning hut
the silver mist wrapped around the word
as only the fog of a mountain sanatorium can.
With my whole body I stroke the womb of colours.

Friends

My friends lying on straw in the mill
dreamt they would wind up stuffed.
The lamp's moths set ablaze their breath –
coins of disquiet, accursed money enough.

Their horses were so beautiful had they strings
I could have sold them as a violin.
They crushed golden comets in their teeth
when ringlets of blood purled at dawn.

The waterwheel skidded across the gravel on its gears,
the bird killer began the Sabbath day:
"Oh Miss I love you you're dead I love you you're dead
sweeter than dry wood is your skin's soft lay!"

Every thought stirred music in objects,
many died by harmony, sweetly stifled –
my friends lying on straw in the mill
dreamt they would wind up stuffed.

Song of Winter

There comes a gentle devil with a lyre that weeps
Oh, how the words' letters still howl in wrath
It's a sign that long bone-carts still sweep
Through violet-blue corridors in the earth.

Can't you hear the olive hut bellow
Across the canal? The lockkeeper shouts a word!
There comes a gentle devil, and some fellow
Who follows with the torch he has shouldered.

Why does the widow's mute child stand
In the garden and wait, dressed only in white?
Why is he holding a lantern in his right hand,
Though the light is out? Can't you hear? Who might

They be, those who passed by, the tall men who took
To pounding at the gate with stones? Don't you feel deep
Wonder? Your rooms fill with smoke,
And there comes a gentle devil with a lyre that weeps.

There comes a gentle devil with a lyre that weeps
Oh, how the words' letters still howl in wrath
It's a sign that long bone-carts still sweep
Through violet-blue corridors in the earth.

If the Red Bird

If the red bird sits by the Wall brooding over words
while enormous honeycombs haunt the air,
my love, you will know that the wasp swarm nears the constellation's edge
and at night your kind must go to the gardens with bright lanterns.

If the red bird sits by the Wall brooding over words,
pay heed, I will mistake your shoulders for mist-draped mangers,
pay heed, I will climb to the peak of the village pub's roof
to signal the wolf dens with a pearl-white flag of sea wrack.

If the red bird sits by the Wall brooding over words
and in rooms olive carts are tied to the ceiling beams,
you will hear a purple ocean mist ship beating onwards with a power
       beyond compare
and through the oceans mist the ice cutters' shouts toward the moors.

Light Crossed the False Green

This is the spot where the fool kept watch.
From here I saw time as a gauzy mist swept away
And the tribe of foxes dying on the day of the eclipse.
Suddenly a cry pierced far into the dusk…

It was hot and children let their souls drop on the grass
Lying beside women's bodies soft as buffalo tongues.
Men brought dark water in hollow gourds
A sign that at the borders the law of seasons was propitious.

Suddenly a cry pierced far into the dusk.
His beloved was on her way, the woman forgotten among horses' names,
Her armpits enslaved by the perfume of the flute…
On a distant meadow light crossed the false green.

Addenda

The Expulsion from Poetry

(The Letters to Constantine)

I

I have only one prejudice – reality,
the same as Democritus the materialist who put out his eyes
so they would not hinder his research undertaken with the mind's eye,
but it's been left for me to catch sight of mankind's huge yellow ear
like a sheep carcass floating on the waters of a swamp
among white calcareous rocks and rustling stands of reeds.
Night after night with my hearing jammed uselessly in my ears like a blind
       man's cane
I feel memory's rifts,
for no rat creeps out, no meadow mouse,
not even a cockroach, the only thing that manages to find its way is my
       voice
from which the word rises up like a snake from its egg and rushes at the
       named object
filling it with sores and meanings.
– Ay, sentences, sentences, dismal marshes inside man's head!
(Hee-hee, my Psyche laughs, hee-hee, for such times as these eyes and
       plague
are equally useful, since, when everything can be said out loud,
nobody chooses words with care any longer!)

Then inspiration's finger presses down my tongue and makes me stammer.
I can scarcely find my way in this whitish haze
that smells of yeast, reaching from martyr to hero,
and my heart is torn apart in the box of my chest, caught between tremors
       of every kind
like a woman's womb at the clear time of puberty.
I hear only my mouth gurgling like a cracked pipe
while the nape of my neck flutters behind me like an empty sleeve
while at its end my head spreads out flatter and flatter like my palm
slapping the lustre of a stone.

II

Who is crazy enough to raise a monument to truth
in the narrow gap between the language of history and the language of
        memory
before putting a bristly wig of pig hair
directly on the heart's skin, the better to
discipline the blood?
For how many does self-consciousness seem too baggy a coat,
how many wear it only in night's intimacy like pyjamas?
Beware, so frequently the senses offer a kind of gala spectacle of
        perception of the world.
In various ways each part of the body exhibits decency,
and courtesy confers a unity on visions;
from the lips hangs a song as delicate as a cotton thread
(about someone who lives on a vacant plot of ground full of flowers
and is happy that his hair grows from his own head).
Hence the cold order of indifference, the frozen connections between
        things,
can often be termed – discipline.
But faced with a fly accidentally crushed on the sheet of paper you're
        writing your poem on,
the muscles of your face quiver, your eyes turn soft like two balls of wool,
a bitter smile follows as fear degenerates into fear's ecstasy…
The death of small many-legged creatures, you tell yourself, makes you
        feel that way.
But poetry refuses to enter the poem
when a reddish stain, almost dry, rules the middle of your sheet of paper,
two little wings and a couple of fly legs.

III

Poetry maintains the balance between mind and body.

I sit with my eyes fixed on the wall. If I truly loved myself less,
I would put out my eyes and cling to the wall with my empty sockets as
        with a pair of glass cups.
Then you'd say: a contemplative nature is like a swinging door between
        rooms.
And you'd giggle like beautiful women who, whenever their predictions
        come true,
have a crisis of maturity.
Look, what already has been teems with meanings. No older than
seventeen, I had an idea for a poem:
the statue of the poet made out of a slab of bread, hanging from a rope
at a factory gate; with a penknife lovers carve on the poet's chest – for
        example,
GHIȚĂ + MONY = LOVE.
Later on: I see lights in the steam from my hands.
Later on: my finger follows a peppercorn in a wine glass.
Then one winter you arrive
and you give these words to me:
We pass from one year to the next as if from room to room, this is how we
        grow old.

.   .   .   .

I walk around the city, cobwebs stuffed in my mouth.

IV

I shoulder the standard of solitude and don't take it where there's pleasure.
Sometimes I stop and proclaim:
"Live your life by the rules of grammar!"
I travel on and the rustling shores of my body sound empty in the air.
Now I sing:
>You are, my love, a nosegay of roses.
>A nosegay of sweet roses.

I know too much about myself; thank God my hands have grown not very
>far from my neck, thank God

my nerves don't dangle from the ceiling of my head like lamps in a pub,
>thank God

destiny doesn't wail inside me supposing itself in a wedding dress.
Now I sing:
>You are, my love, a nosegay of roses.
>A nosegay of sweet roses.

Lonely like a scream in a hospital courtyard.
I have rolled down enough streets, rolled like a piece of candy.
I climb the house and put my lips to the chimney top as to a trumpet's
>mouthpiece

and howl through the smoke:
"Live your life by the rules of grammar!"
Now I sing:
>You are, my love, a nosegay of roses.
>A nosegay of sweet roses.

V

I see lights in the steam from my hands: the time has come for me also to
      scream
under the bellies of symbols.
The same as in childhood, when Mother made an ear out of rags, patted
      me and said,
"It's yours. Scream into it till you tear it to tatters!"
Here I am, I have come back home and I can hear the fortune-tellers
      snickering under my window,
short and shrill like a girl.
I eavesdrop and giggle.
Madness sits at my work table. Looks up from my poems with yellow eyes:
"Don't be annoyed, I'll just join you at your table, taste whatever I taste,
      then leave!"
Madness smiles a bittersweet smile. Scratches the chair with a fingernail.
.   .   .   .

Now what I want to do is to scream with somebody else's mouth, even a
      deaf mute's.

from
THE POEM
THAT CANNOT BE
UNDERSTOOD
(1993)

The Poet. A Child's Testimony.

Night was falling when I propped the ladder beneath his window.
He sat in the middle of the room, speaking softly.
Two dry twigs, two rotten logs hovered above his head, in flames,
pebbles in piles on the floor,
mortar in a little silver box.
Much later I heard a faint rustle by the door,
and with great haste, right in the middle of his table, he began to build
a white wall almost to the ceiling.
Just before dawn he stopped and sang a song that blackened the wall.
A kind of creature, like a monkey, appeared from under his coat
and, chattering, jumped all around the room.
Then his words inflated like balloons,
his querulous, calumnious words in every colour
surrounded the monkey and made it shut its mouth.
When I went away, only his head could be seen among the words,
the head of a very old man yelling something incomprehensible
in the midst of a herd of buffalo.

A Group of Old Men Near the Poet's House

For a week he has been holed up in the cellar, digging.
(This news has us gathered here
the way bits of bone clump together in a jellied soup.)
At first we heard laughter and muffled blows,
so we pressed our ears to the walls,
but the walls of his house, soft and warm, twitched like a cow's skin.
Ever since, we have been leaning quietly against the fence,
and at night we have maybe lit a fire –
the nights get cold this time of year.
(Fear holds us gathered here
the way bits of bone clump together in a jellied soup,
fear is this sheet of black
we take turns hiding our head under.)
We should also report that he came out yesterday, a sack of earth over his
        shoulder,
and had not yet thrown it down
when a thin pink tongue wrapped itself around his waist
and yanked him back inside, sack and all,
the door slamming behind him with a quick gulp.
Now, look, here he is, you too can see him, he's coming out smiling,
heading straight toward us, a rusty bucket in his hand,
and he shows us at its bottom, among the yellow clods, among the
        pebbles –
how it leaps, it jerks about, it spins in a frenzy –
a tiny eye, black and evil.

Orpheus

I turned my head and looked back – that's what I should have done at the
      very beginning.
Through air thick as sour cream, I alone hollowed out a tunnel and saw:
far into the distance, screen after screen,
and above each of them dozens of heads – hers – held between hands
in black gloves. Oh, those dozens of small round heads, heads
like copper coins.

I don't mean to lie. The god himself came along, too.
He had no face, only a cast-iron slab, flat and compact,
like the door of a wood stove. And two hands, similarly in black elbow-
      length gloves,
stuck out from his head, waving with a sort of elegance, as if someone,
a showgirl, were drowning in him as in a well.

Now, while I sit in my easy chair, on my knees a fat candle as round as her
      body,
and listen as a mouse digs a tunnel through the wax,
gnawing the wick until it crawls out in the flame and there starts
      squeaking,
now I can see everything with great lucidity.

Glass fingers on a glass bottle.
A glass bottle between glass fingers.
Wine-dark lips on the wine.
Wine on wine-dark lips.

What I should have done at the very beginning.

A Life Ruined by Poetry

Poisonous poem, sing as you press your disgusting lips
       to my lips.
Your scabby words, scrofulous, louse-infested,
       your whoring words
bite young maidens' breasts, bite the grey hair
       on men's chests.
You bitch's whelp, you have crippled my loves,
exhausted my life, squandered the honey of my days
       in a language of shamelessness.

Neither the critics, nor the literary magazines, nor the super-subtle
       academicians will put an end to you,
no, only the flayers, the rat-catchers, the National Health Officers,
       the epidemiologists, the Securitate, the dermatologists, the
       gynaecologists – for them
in turn I'll be a chance to help serve the public good.
       But as for me,
you have exhausted my life, squandered the honey of my days
       in a language of shamelessness.

Song at the Hospital Gate

This white spot is a window-pane of white.
This white spot is the blade of a knife.
Only a spot of white, only a spot of white
keeps whirling before my eyes.

This red spot is foliage of red.
This red spot is my tormented heart.
Only a spot of red, only a spot of red
keeps whirling before my eyes.

This yellow spot is a harbinger of madness.
This yellow spot is madness breathing down my neck.
Only a spot of yellow, only a spot of yellow
keeps whirling before my eyes.

Gentle angel, royal blossom,
from my ways snatch me pell-mell,
caress me, wash me,
and in an empty white room
make me ring like a bell.

The Poem that Cannot be Understood

I work on the poem that cannot be understood.
It's a shiny black rock
from which the wiry hair of thirty-three wild beasts suddenly starts to
       grow;
it's the green swamp reclaiming the town square –
among its reeds a lonely fox barks softly, submissively;
it's the wooden bride (oh, the marvellous wooden bride!) – the pale blue
       dress, the herb-filled mouth,
the whimpering that coats the window like lichen;
it's the hole in the sky and the cloud of blood snarling in the hole in the
       sky;
it's the murder of crows joyously wheeling about my forehead,
the black frost of my forehead: the tongue in my mouth ice cold, on
       the brink of shattering, like a medal bestowed by God on the
       prophets;
it's the wine that turns to sand in your mouth.

Oh, the times when our house burst into bloom on the shores of slippery
       language!
On words creeping forth from the caves of speech…
When the words creeping forth from the caves of speech
climbed the walls like snails…
Then the sweet, dusty archives of the asylums
where I studied signs contrived by lunatics,
where I compiled their vast history
which, written in those same desiccated signs,
I myself never could read.
That is why I included it in the poem that cannot be understood.
I see a round head, like a golden balloon, drifting further and further away
       high over the book shelves.

I hear the ocean surf pounding against the walls of a tall yellow warehouse,
and getting old, nearly hunchbacked,
my halo folded and tucked under my arm,
I stand in line, behind hundreds and hundreds of people,

in order to see, at least at the end of my days,
the poem that heals,
the poem that cannot be understood.

Poem

Just a single sentence, white cartilage stretched taut from mouth to mouth,
a coiled rope in the lungs –
this is what God showed me in a dream, on the tenth day of the month,
when the wind blew trash into the sky.

The spirit kept grinning from the brain's periphery, like a wet monkey
come out of a swamp, shivering in the cold air,
trying to scamper up a birch tree –
this is what God showed me in a dream, on the tenth day of the month,
when the wind blew trash into the sky.

A unique sense of hearing, an endless white tunnel, an ox bone from
       ear to ear
and the warm marrow pressing under your temples, the rustle of the
       intimate lingerie of abstractions –
this is what God showed me in a dream, on the tenth day of the month,
when the wind blew trash into the sky.

The spirit, wanton in the heat of its potency,
became acrid smoke spewing forth from the broken windows,
a thick smoke-ring in the yard outside the deserted barracks
where I dozed on a crimson throne, at the tip of a breast of yellow earth.
Rusted Red-Army buttons littered the grass, glittered like hot embers.
This is what God showed me in a dream, on the tenth day of the month,
when the wind blew trash into the sky.

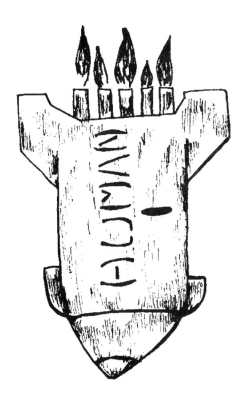

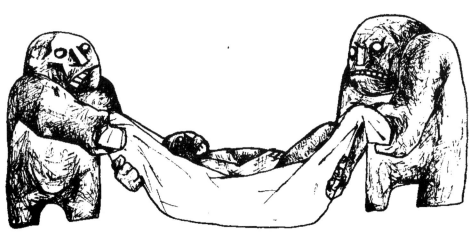

from
THE ALCOHOL BOOK
(2010)

The Alcoholics' Poem

Alas, the poor, poor alcoholics,
nobody ever has a good word for them!
Especially in the morning, when they stagger along the walls
and sometimes fall to their knees, like the clumsy ABCs
scrawled by a schoolboy's hand.

God alone, in His great beneficence, causes a pub to manifest itself along
        their way,
for Him it's a snap, the way a child
slides a matchbox along with a finger. So hardly
do they reach the end of the road when, around the corner,
where a moment before nothing was – slap-bang – like a rabbit,
a pub hops out in front of them and stops.
Then a bashful light dawns in their eyes.
They are drenched in sweat from so much happiness.

Before noon the city looks purple.
Before noon it's autumn three times, it's spring three times,
the birds fly to warmer climes and back three times.
And they gab on and on about life. About life
in general, even young alcoholics express a warm, responsible viewpoint.
If they stutter and stumble,
it's not because they propose terribly profound ideas,
but because inspired by youth
they succeed in saying truly moving things.

But God, in His great beneficence, does not stop there!
Directly, He pokes a finger through the wall of Heaven
and invites the alcoholics to take a peek.
(Oh, where can such happiness be found for any human creature!)
And even though they have the shakes so bad they can't manage to see
        more than a little patch of grass,
still, it's something supernatural.
Until one of them awakens and spoils everything. He says:
"Soon, soon, night must fall,

then we'll rest and find peace!"
They stand up from their tables one by one,
wipe their clammy lips with a handkerchief,
and feel very, very ashamed.

The Old Lover and the Young Lady

My eyes saw red, only
a red mountain as I left the bar,
for it was cold and the air damp, a really bad thing for asthmatics.
The worse my cough, the more tenderly she held my arm,
tender because of the cold.
When I stopped coughing, I strutted like a stork.
It felt like my head was in a jar, and
I was not very steady on my feet.

I stepped between the puddles, declaiming Pound
as best I remembered, a hand in the air rather theatrically:
"If a man would be a lover
                    he may walk on the Scythian coast,
No barbarian would go to the extent of doing him harm,…
Cupid will carry lighted torches before him
                    and keep mad dogs off him."
And she, in a nurse's voice, "Quiet, be quiet,
you'll start coughing again!"…

My God, I have no idea where they appeared from!
Two on one side, two on the other.
One of them, the one with a mauve hedgehog on his head, says,
"Did'ya see that dirty old man, how he pawed her under the table
and how he made her head spin with Plato's gibberish?"
Another of them, like a child, more petulant:
"When I think his shrivelled lips will suck her breasts,
round like ripe peaches, ptooey, I could puke!
Now, let's give the pussy some fresh milk!"
Then the one with the hedgehog on his head:
"Yeah, sweet dreams for Gramps,
time for beddy-byes!"
He smacked me hard.
And she, like a cat sewn to my sleeve.

My God, I saw only the pavement, it moved,
it rose above me, it wrapped me around like a wet blanket.
Then buildings upside down.
A dark puddle covered me like a pillow over my ears.
Hush-a-bye in a field of flowers!
When I came to, I tried to push the blanket off but couldn't.
And hush-a-bye in a field of flowers again, and next a slap,
she crying and kissing me, an eye turning black and blue,
her lips as if bitten by mice, her dress torn:
"Quiet, be quiet, you'll start coughing again!"
It was a struggle but I stood, while she plucked her pink tights from the
            fence
and stuffed them in her purse.

Now, not quite twenty-five, she seems an old lady:
dark circles under her eyes,
forehead wrinkled, lips creased, breasts fallen.
There's nothing I can do if she has set her mind on growing old
and grows old according to her plan.
"In two years," she says, "love will make me just like you,
and you'll never again be ashamed with me
at a bar in the evening!"
And I call her slut. But then angel.
And she, in a nurse's voice,
"Quiet, be quiet, you'll start coughing again!"

A Hint of the Sea in a Small Pub

She sits on his knee. At each movement
the chair screeches under them like a seagull.
"Hell of a life," he says from time to time,
but the bearded man opposite him cannot hear.
(Elbow on the table, his hand like a sea shell cupping an ear).
The bearded man hears only the roar of waves and, gently, together with
      the table,
he rocks to the cadence of the breakers.

Now the man's hand weighs heavy on her thigh.
The bearded man bends and spits as if he had swigged sand.
The hand creeps higher and higher. Now, through her dress, with his
      thumb he feels
her rounded pubis, hard as a wooden egg.
"Hell of a life," he says. And in a while,
"You're heavy, wife. Shift to the other knee!"

She stands up, while the bearded man undresses her with his gaze.
She knows it, her nipples sting. As if he had set her dress on fire
with a cigarette lighter. Then rough fingers
squeeze the soft flesh between the thighs. Once. That's all.

The bearded man stares into the distance. He is watching the red curtain
      that drapes
the entrance to the WC. When the curtain moves, there's a heavy seaweed
      smell.
The curtain flutters like shreds of a cloud far out at sea at dawn.
"Hell of a life," the man says to the woman.
The bearded man hears that. "The sun hasn't risen,"
the bearded man says, "our sun hasn't yet risen."

Dark Song

I sing the dark force in my mind,
at the command of the dark force in my mind.
Among ice teas I sing a cold dry song,
a little ditty that paralyses the imagination
just as icebergs paralyse smells.
Now I feel at peace, my mind is clear,
clear and sterile.
And while I sing, images clot like blood
above white cups.
Smells wear thinner and thinner like cigarette paper
and stick to ice-cubes.
Like stamps.

The sun is high, the grass rotten –
the time is ripe to mow!

Powerful is the song about the dark force in my mind.
The swamp boils under the floor, roiling under thin planks.
My house starts to sink.
A swarm of flies is all I see. Through black flies I catch a glimpse of
willows crouched about my window like green pubic hair.
Cattails, reeds and sedge block the pane. The water sways gently.
Duckweed and water hemlock creep softly over the sill.
A water snake, too.
Through the glass, the head with yellow flowers draws near
the head with grey hair. And mud. Lake shells faintly grinding in the walls.
Then mud.

The sun is high, the grass rotten –
the time is ripe to mow!

I switch on the light and dress in a black shirt.
Over the roof, somewhere up above, the swamp boils.
Across the century, heavy trucks grind their gears.
Red tractors plough.

The roof tiles ring like the bells of Heaven.
My mind is clearer and clearer,
more and more sterile.
I have descended to the depths of the dark force in my mind.
I am the dark force in the mind of the dark force in my mind.
I issue a command: Sing the dark force in your mind!

The sun is high, the grass rotten –
the time is ripe to mow!

The Glass

It's an enchanted night.
The moon trembles in my glass, round and yellow.
I stick my finger in the glass.
Next I stick my arm in the glass, as far as the elbow.
Then I stick my arm in the glass, as far as the shoulder.
The vodka is ice cold.
On the bottom of the glass, there's a large stone slab.
There are dead leaves and dark roots.
There's a torn rubber boot, too.
On the bottom of the glass, there's also a rusty stove.
I stick my head in the glass.
The vodka is ice cold.
I open my eyes in the glass.
In the glass, I can see well even without eyeglasses.
I say out loud, "All is dream and harmony."
The stone slab is white with thin red veins.
Now I notice the Beast.
Now I hear it purring low, like a cat.
I see its blue legs.
I see its fearsome tail jutting out from under the stone slab.
A crystal-clear spring flows beside the stone slab.
It whispers over the gravel.
At its edges the grass is always green.
Delicate flowers grow in the grass.
In the spring pool swim children as small as dolls.
They swim with incredibly quick movements.
They swim in little dresses and shirts and trousers in jolly colours.
They are the little angels of the glass.
The little angels of the glass don't bite or do harm to anyone.
I feel like vomiting from pity, I feel like vomiting from sadness.
I feel like vomiting when I realise I might swallow one of the little angels.
I feel like crying at the thought that he would suddenly be so lonely.
Crying at the thought that he would sob all night, just like me.
Crying at the thought that he could be singing nursery rhymes inside me.
He could sing in a high, shrill voice, "Spring is coming, sweet spring!"

With my nails dug into the Beast's back, I plunge toward the bottom of the
      glass.
A stone slab is there, with thin red veins.
Now I lie on the slab with thin red veins.
Far away, somewhere in the glass, a dog keeps barking.
It's autumn.
It's the day of the eclipse.
The round yellow moon trembles in the glass.
Through a piece of glass smoky from a candle flame, I see a big black fly
      buzzing around the bulb.
With my nails dug into the Beast's back, I drag its head out from under the
      stone.
Its terrifying back snakes like a train through mountains.
With my nails, I drag the Beast's locomotive out from under the stone
      slab.
The little angels of the glass hold hands and dance gently in a circle.
The little angels dance and sing all around us.
"All is dream and harmony."
The Beast has one eye of my mother's and one eye of my father's.
In the glass, I can see well even without my eyeglasses.
I read in my mother's eye, "My son, when will you finally understand?"
I read in my father's eye, "My son, when will you finally understand?"
The glass squeezes my forehead like an iron band.
It hurts.
My head bangs against the walls: this side and that, this side and that.
The little angel of the glass sobs with pain.
The little angel of the glass sings inside me in a high, shrill voice, "Spring
      is coming, sweet spring!"
"All is dream and harmony."

The Tunnel

for my friend, Ioan Groșan

We were sitting at a table, the waiter nowhere in sight.
And we were sad, lost in thought,
because we knew we didn't have a lot longer to live.
Suddenly, our image was cut into the wall facing the street,
as if, then and there, a stare that would not brook refusal
had to look at us right away, as if
a child had cut our shape into a piece of wood
with a small fretsaw.
Then our image was thrust
into the bus just going by,
holding it in place for nearly a minute,
until the image crossed through it.
Then our image pierced the building on the other side of the road,
passing through closets and chairs,
through children and housewives.
Our image sitting at a table, the waiter nowhere in sight,
penetrated the mountains like a tunnel far into the distance,
pierced the salty air above the sea,
a Turkish ship and a fish.
The image bored through the desert
like a glass tunnel.
Mother felt a twinge in her chest, too,
when our image sitting at a table, the waiter nowhere in sight,
crossed through her,
our dog barked,
and the cock on the fence crew,
pierced through.
Slowly, with difficulty, our image once again cut through the city
and the opposite wall of the pub, and our image
fell upon us,
without our being a part of it.

At the Table by the Window

"Here a man can cry and smoke *won-der-ful-ly*!"
I told the bartender, because, so many times, at the table by the window,
I've sat and sighed very late into the night,
thinking that you're so far, my love, so very far away,
and I will never see you again.

And he, "a face smeared with oil like an iron lock,"
huffed and fogged over a glass.
"My dear sir, we will be most honoured if you cry here among us,
we will be honoured if you smoke! And so we can cry together,
in your honour, I'll even give myself a slap!
In your honour, I'll give myself another!
Nevertheless, in our Romanian culture there's too much crying,
for, if you would be so kind as to agree with me, we're a very weepy
   people!"
His old angel's head set slowly among the glasses –
like the moon among snow-covered hills.

The pub was packed: three or four men at each table,
hunched like badgers over ashtrays.
(Faces twisted with pain,
silent as in dream).

Soon it was midnight, soon midnight was long past,
and the humps of their backs twitched, bobbed up and down,
as if each had a turkey under his coat,
its claws jabbing between his ribs. The bartender walked from one table to
   another, singing,
"How can I ever forget you, forget you, forget you
when your kisses are so sweet!"
Then the turkeys stuck their heads out from under collars, like snakes,
like flags with red tassels beside each ear, ugly flags, flags with beaks,
and a murmur like low gobbling travelled from table to table:
"*Glu-glu-glu*, Maria, why did you leave me?
Glu-glu-glu, Maria, why did you cheat on me?

Glu-glu-glu, Maria, I did time in the clink for you!
Glu-glu-glu, Maria, you left me with five kids, what should I do?"

Every table was
like a house
with three or four chimneys smoking.
We all drank, elbows on the roof.

Under the ceiling, squeaking,
a fan wound our lungs into a grey ball.

Tears and ashes in ashtrays, murky water.

As I sat facing the wall,
I began to laugh,
and I pointed my finger up above and said,
"The work has stopped! All the work has stopped!"
Going out into the street, I looked at the sky:
the sky was a construction site hurriedly abandoned at the
        coming of winter.

The Author

Ion Mureșan is one of Romania's most honoured poets, although he has published only three collections of poetry. *The Book of Winter* (*Cartea de iarnă*, 1981) established his fame as a kind of 'poet's poet' of 'fiery' and 'metaphysical' poetry; it appeared at the beginning of the last, and most difficult, decade of communist control of Romania. An elemental and riddling collection, *The Book of Winter* assumes the primal importance of the poet in interpreting and cleansing society and cultural attitudes. The collection was awarded the prize of the Romanian Writers' Union for a first book of poetry. It appears in its entirety in this selection of Mureșan's work.

Twelve years later, *The Poem That Cannot Be Understood* (*Poemul care nu poate fi înțeles*, 1993) deepened and extended the poet's reputation as a representative voice of his generation, a traditionalist who develops a kind of cerebral and finely wrought, powerfully expressionistic poetry that delves into the fears, neuroses, and displacements of the interior reality of the poet's representative lyric persona. The collection develops more prominently the notion of poetry being intrinsically spiritual and even dangerous in its intensity and irony. It won the poetry prize of the Writers' Union.

The Alcohol Book (*Cartea Alcool*, 2010) was published 17 years later, to immediate acclaim in Romania. It represents a change in Mureșan's style, with a more transparent, discursive, and narrative poetry. It was named Best Poetry Volume of the Year with an award from the Romanian Ministry of Culture. To Mureșan, who has noted that one can sometimes "find God in a pub rather than in a church," the symbols of alcohol and drink are both biographical and suggestive, with religious implications. Poems from *The Alcohol Book* as well as from *The Poem That Cannot Be Understood* are included in this University of Plymouth Press volume.

Mureșan has also written short stories, *The Sunday of Madness* (*Duminica turbării*, 1994), and a book of essays on revisiting literature he read as a child, *The Lost Book – a Poetics of Traces* (*Cartea pierdută – o poetică a urmei*, 1998). This latter was honoured by the Cluj branch of the Romanian Writers' Union. He has also put into print a volume of plays for children, *Carnival in the Meadow* (*Carnavalul din poiană*, 2004, written with his wife Ana).

Born on January 9, 1955, in Vultureni, a village in the county of Cluj in Transylvania, Mureșan lives today in the city of Cluj, where he works as a journalist and edits the cultural magazine *Verso*.

The Translators

Adam J. Sorkin recently published *A Path to the Sea*, poems by Liliana Ursu in joint translations by Ursu, Sorkin, and Tess Gallagher (Pleasure Boat Studios); *Media and Her War Machines*, poems by Ioan Flora translated with Alina Cărăc (University of New Orleans Press); and *My Dog – the Soul*, poems by Floarea Țuțuianu translated with Irma Giannetti (Cold Hub Press), all in 2011. His other books of translation include *Memory Glyphs*, a collection of three Romanian prose poets, Cristian Popescu, Iustin Panța and Radu Andriescu (Twisted Spoon, 2009), and Ruxandra Cesereanu's *Crusader-Woman*, translated mainly with Cesereanu (Black Widow, 2008), and he is the main translator (with the poet) of *Rock and Dew: Selected Poems* by Carmen Firan (The Sheep Meadow Press, 2010). Sorkin's awards number among them the *International Quarterly* Crossing Boundaries Award and the Kenneth Rexroth Memorial Translation Prize, as well as arts grants and publication support from the National Endowment for the Arts (USA), Rockefeller Foundation, Academy of American Poets, Arts Council of England, New York State Arts Council, Romanian Cultural Institute, and Fulbright, Soros and Witter Bynner Foundations. His Bloodaxe books, Liliana Ursu's *The Sky Behind the Forest* (1997), translated with Ursu and Tess Gallagher, and Ioana Ieronim's *The Triumph of the Water Witch* (2000), translated with Ieronim, were shortlisted for the Oxford-Weidenfeld Prize. He teaches at Penn State Brandywine, where he holds the title of Distinguished Professor of English.

Lidia Vianu, a poet, novelist, critic, and translator, is Professor of Contemporary British Literature at the University of Bucharest, where she is also Director of CTITC (Centre for the Translation and Interpretation of the *Contemporary Text*) and editor of the online publishing press *Contemporary Literature Press* (http://mttlc.ro/editura) and the online review, *Translation Café* (http://revista.mttlc.ro). She has been a Fulbright lecturer at the University of California Berkeley and SUNY Binghamton. Her literary criticism includes *The AfterMode: Significant Choices in Contemporary British Fiction* (2010); *The Desperado Age: British Literature at the Start of the Third Millennium* (2004); *Alan Brownjohn and the Desperado Age* (2003); *British Desperadoes at the Turn of the Millennium* (1999); as well as *T. S. Eliot: An Author for All Seasons*. She has also published two books of interviews, *Censorship in Romania* (Central European University Press, 1997) and *Desperado Essay-Interviews* (Bucharest University Press, 2006); a novel, *Prisoner in the Mirror* (1993); three poetry collections, *1, 2, 3* (1997), *Moderato 7* (1998), *Very* (2001); English learning manuals; and seven edited anthologies. This is her eighteenth book of translation.

Sorkin and Vianu won the Poetry Society's 2005 Corneliu M. Popescu Prize for European Poetry Translation for Marin Sorescu's *The Bridge* (Bloodaxe, 2004). Their translation of Mircea Ivănescu's *lines poems poetry* was published by University of Plymouth Press in 2009, followed by Ioan Es. Pop's *No Way Out of Hadesburg and other Poems* in 2010. Ivănescu's *lines poems poetry* was shortlisted for the Poetry Society's 2011 Popescu Translation Prize.

Acknowledgments

Adam J. Sorkin expresses gratitude to the University College of the Pennsylvania State University, to Penn State Brandywine, and to the Penn State Institute for the Arts and Humanities for their support of his work on this book.

Some of the poems in this book were translated previously with two other collaborators: seven poems with Liviu Bleoca in *Transylvanian Voices: An Anthology of Contemporary Poets of Cluj-Napoca* (Iaşi, Romania: Romanian Cultural Foundation, 1994, 1997), and three with Georgiana Farnoaga in *Day After Night: Twenty Romanian Poets for the Twenty-First Century* (Norcross, GA: Criterion Publishing, 1999). Although not consciously echoed, phrasing was borrowed from these earlier versions, a sign hopefully not of a translator's limitations but of his consistency.

Hardback edition first published in the United Kingdom in 2011 by University of Plymouth Press, Roland Levinsky Building, Drake Circus, Plymouth, Devon, PL4 8AA, United Kingdom.

ISBN 978-1-84102-213-0

A CIP catalogue record of this book is available from the British Library

Translation: Adam J. Sorkin and Lidia Vianu
Publisher: Paul Honeywill
Publishing Assistant: Charlotte Carey
Series Art Director: Sarah Chapman
Romanian Art Consultant: Simona Vilău
Romanian Cultural Institute: Mihaela Ghiţă
Editorial Advisors: Cristina Sandru, Dennis Deletant and Adina Bradeanu

Typeset by University of Plymouth Press in Janson 10/14pt
Printed and bound by Short Run Press, Exeter, EX2 7LW

Visit www.uppress.co.uk/romanian.htm

Published with the support of the Romanian Cultural Institute

NATIONAL BOOK CENTRE — ROMANIAN CULTURAL INSTITUTE

FSC Mixed Sources
Product group from well-managed forests, controlled sources and recycled wood or fibre
www.fsc.org Cert no. SGS-COC-005998
© 1996 Forest Stewardship Council

20 ROMANIAN WRITERS SERIES

Twenty of Romania's most influential and award-winning authors are launched by UPP in the series 20 Romanian Writers. Romanian arts have long been unknown in the West and this series aims to make a lasting contribution to the canon of Eastern European literature.

These works have been translated into English for the first time; the collection captures Romania's rich cultural diversity and artistic heritage. Selected by an independent Romanian jury of editors, academics and publishers, the series showcases the most notable Romanian novels, essays, poetry, short prose and philosophy of the 20th and 21st centuries.

Each volume is edited and comes with a substantial introduction that contextualises the work not only within Romanian, but Eastern European and Anglo-American traditions. Texts are complemented with a 16 page full colour supplement provided by some of Romania's leading contemporary visual artists. 20 Romanian Writers is a landmark collection of the very best Romanian writing. The titles published in this series so far are:

The Cinematography Caravan

IOAN GROȘAN

A black comedy set in 1960's Romania: a Stalinist propaganda film truck rumbles into a forgotten Transylvanian village. The occupants of the village believe in the traditional values of Church and God and are in no mood to participate, placing obstacles in the way of the Cinematography Caravan crew. The resultant humour is deliberately provincial as the villagers find their own unique ways of dealing with them while they're in town.

ISBN 978-1-84102-205-5

Lines Poems Poetry

MIRCEA IVĂNESCU

Ivănescu's poetry represents the achievement of a little-known master. Centring on a wide cast of characters including his alter ego 'mopete', Ivănescu's idiosyncratic, lyrical sensibility offers allusive, comic and elegiac meditations on our common lot.

Ivănescu's *Lines Poems Poetry* was shortlisted for the Poetry Society's 2011 Popescu Translation Prize.

ISBN 978-1-84102-217-8

Occurrence in the Immediate Unreality

MAX BLECHER

This autobiographical fiction offers an intimate and unsettling account of Blecher's ideas of self-identity and the body. He explores the 'crisis of unreality' in relation to the human condition and shares his adolescent experiences of physical infirmity, social isolation and sexual awakening.

ISBN 978-1-84102-207-9

Six Maladies of the Contemporary Spirit

CONSTANTIN NOICA

In this unique work, Noica analyses history, culture and the individual in what he describes as the fundamental precariousness of being. 'Maladies' of the spirit are no longer debilitating, but creative for our European interest in change, unity, and diversity.

ISBN 978-1-84102-203-1

The Băiuţ Alley Lads

FILIP AND MATEI FLORIAN

Two brothers, Filip and Matei, are growing up in a totalitarian society. Everyday life is recounted through their young eyes. Their world is filled with characters from children's television, broadcast by the official communist media, alongside magazines and cinema. 'Joe Lemonade', 'Giani Morandi' and 'Brooslee' accentuate the absurdity and grotesqueness of their surroundings.

The brothers become close through a shared love of football, supporting the same team, Dinamo Bucureşti. Ultimately, *The Băiuţ Alley Lads* is a novel about miracles that take place within a nightmare, regardless of whether they occur in an obscure lane in an obscure district of a country kept in obscurity by communist dictatorship.

ISBN 978-1-84102-267-3

No Way Out of Hadesburg and Other Poems

IOAN ES. POP

In Romania under communist rule, forbidden to write but allowed to work as a builder on Ceauşescu's palace, Ioan Es. Pop lived alone in a bachelor block. His poetry is an autobiographical account of this time: a life with no way out. Having originally been a teacher in a village that he later gives the fictional name of Hadesburg, Pop's writing expresses his response to such a life. The world of the poems is a closed, boundless, imaginary space charged with dramatic intensity and tempered by a bitter-sweet, compassionate, existential angst.

ISBN 978-1-84102-209-3

STELIAN TĂNASE

Stelian Tănase's books explore the politics of the totalitarian state. He is an historical authority on the communist period in Romania. *Auntie Varvara's Clients* brings to life documents discovered in the archives of the pre-communist secret police, the Siguranţa (nicknamed 'Auntie Varvara'). This extensive work reveals a regime reliant on secrecy. The narrative changes tense unannounced, giving a surreal, filmic quality to the writing. Tănase takes us from the early days of illegal membership of the communist underground, at the end of the First World War, to their eventual rise to power and the struggle for supremacy.

ISBN 978-1-84102-221-5

Who Won the World War of Religions?

DANIEL BĂNULESCU

Contemporary madness in its entirety is summarised in Daniel Bănulescu's play, set in an asylum populated with 12 dangerous madmen who are divided as believers of the four major religions. This is theatre in a world governed by insanity; as Dan Stanca remarks, the play could be set anywhere – in Piteşti, in the Siberian Gulag, in a Nazi concentration camp, Maoist or Khmer Rouge extermination camp, and, even, in one of the CIA's secret prisons... This is the principal merit and black humour of the play.

ISBN 978-1-84102-212-3

RĂZVAN PETRESCU

Regulars in a village bar chew over rumours of the Chernobyl disaster. The perpetrator of the first murder tries to tell the court his side of the story. A resident in a block of flats is disconcerted to find his neighbours gradually falling victim to a mysterious epidemic. A chance encounter in the Bucharest Metro sparks an explosion of increasingly bizarre storytelling... Rich in invention and stylistic variety, combining sharp observation with playful fantasy, ironic detachment with an underlying sense of tragedy, Răzvan Petrescu's stories offer a series of variations on the human condition in a tragicomic key. *Small Changes in Attitude* contains a selection from his first three books of short stories *The Summer* Garden (1989), *Eclipse* (1993), and *One Friday Afternoon* (1997).

ISBN 978-1-84102-214-7

NICOLAE MANOLESCU

Inspired by the combination of political intrigue and love contained within the belles-lettres of the great French novelists, Manolescu uses this recipe to tell the story of a great love. Cristina Chevereşan considers French Themes as 'love declared or merely suggested, patient and durable, arousing the aromas of French perfumes but also a reading in culture and civilization'.

Manolescu has been a member of the Romanian Academy since 1998. He is a critic and literary historian who was elected President of the Writers' Union of Romania in 2005. In 2006 he was appointed Romanian Ambassador to UNESCO.

ISBN 978-1-84102-208-6

ION MUREȘAN

There is at once an enigmatic and original character to the poetic language of Ion Mureșan, who concerns himself through this anthology with the political nature of Romanian poetry. Mureșan's poetry draws upon Transylvanian legends to explore the way the communist manipulation and monopoly of truth leaves the individual powerless. By regaining individual thoughts, through his poetry there is a promise of salvation which reflects what it is to be Romanian.

He is one of the poets included in the anthology *12 Ecrivains Roumains*, published by Éditions L'Inventaire on the occasion of Les Belles Étrangeres Programme organised by the Centre National du Livre in 2005. Some of his latest poems, *Alcohol* (2010) have been included in this edition.

ISBN 978-1-84102-213-0

MIRCEA CĂRTĂRESCU

Cărtărescu brings together 21 short stories and articles that he wrote mainly for *ELLE* magazine. The protagonist of every story is female, but they are not individual portraits of women – it is a group portrait of womanhood.

His books have received awards from the Romanian Academy, the Writers' Union of Romania, the Moldovan Writers' Union, ASPRO, the Bucharest Association of Writers, the Association of Romanian Publishers, and the *Cuvîntul, Ateneu, Flacăra, Tomis* and *Ziarul de Iași* reviews. In France, he has been nominated for the Médicis, Le Meilleur Livre Étranger, and Prix Union Latine. His novel *Nostalgia* won the Giuseppe Acerbi Prize at Castle Goffredo, Italy, in 2005.

ISBN 978-1-84102-206-2

Notes on Romanian Spelling and Pronunciation

As the Romanian spelling system is phonetically based and highly regular, it should not be difficult for the reader to achieve a reasonably accurate pronunciation of the various Romanian names and other words that occur in this book, if the following are borne in mind:

Consonants

c – before *e* or *i* as in 'church', otherwise as in 'coat'
ch (before *e* or *i*) – as English *k* in 'king'
g – before *e* or *i* as in 'gem', otherwise as in 'goat'
gh (before *e* or *i*) – as English *g* in 'get'
j – like the sound represented by *s* in 'measure'
r – pronounced in all positions, slightly rolled.
s – as in 'seat' (never as in 'rose')
ş – as English *sh*
ţ – as English *ts*
Other consonants are pronounced much as in English.

Vowels

a, e, i, o, u: similar to Italian pronunciation, apart from the following:
– final *i* is generally almost silent (as in *Bucureşti*, pronounced bookoo<u>resht</u>)
– *i* before another vowel sounds like English *y* (as in the personal name *Ion*, which sounds like 'yon')
– *o* before *a* sounds like English *w* (as in *Timişoara*, pronounced teemee<u>shwara</u>)
ă – like the *a-* in 'about', or the *-er* in 'mother' (but not so weakly stressed).
â or *î* – something like the *i* in 'fill', but with the tongue further back in the mouth

Stress

In general the contrast between stressed and unstressed syllables is not as strong in Romanian as in English. However there is a tendency, especially in longer words, for the last syllable to receive more stress if the word ends in a consonant, and the penultimate if it ends in a vowel.

James Christian Brown

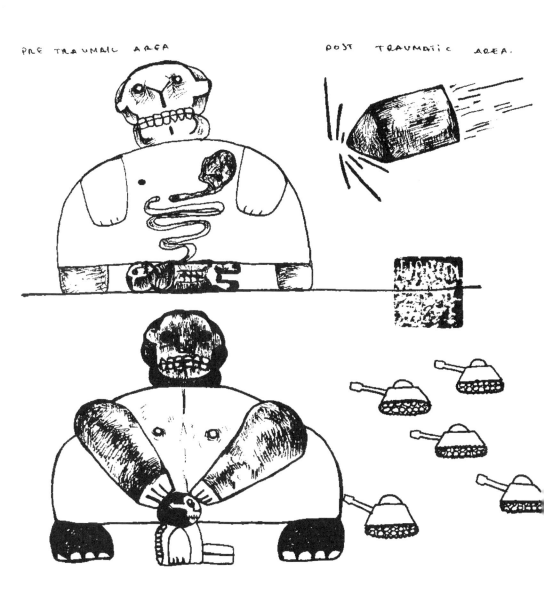